ISBN 0-9548564-5-7

Published by:
Zebra Publishing
7 Gosforth Terrace
South Gosforth
Newcastle upon Tyne
NE3 1RT

For information contact
annie@zebrapublishing.co.uk

Zebra Publishing is a member of
Independent Northern Publishers

For online sales visit
www.northernpublishers.co.uk/publishers/Zebra

Printed and bound by:
Jasprint
Washington
Co Durham

Introduction

Zebra Publishing believes that poetry speaks for Everyman and that there is poetry in all of us. When we're faced with new experiences, from breathtaking joy to heart stopping sorrow we turn to poetry for comfort, for clarity. We find compassion and perspective. We cry. We have a laugh.

In this collection Jeff touches these emotions and many more. Join him on his walk through dictionaries. Sway with him on the terraces following the thrills of his team, observing the heady changes in the city he has grown up in and loved all his life. Meet his ever expanding family. Share his passions. Enjoy a good pint.

Annie Moir

Editor
Zebra Publishing

"Dis poetry is not afraid of going in a book
Still dis poetry needs ears fe hear
An eyes fe have a look"

Benjamin Zephaniah

Doors

A collection by Jeff Price

This book is about doors; some real, some not.

Doors tell me far more about buildings than the bricks and mortar that surround them. They tell me if the building is cared for or if there is a sense of pride. It can make me feel "welcome" or say "keep out". Sometimes it speaks of a glorious past or indicates a listless future.

Most of my life has been spent trying to open doors that have been closed to me. Sometimes I have followed other people, sometimes I tried to find my own way. I love the excitement of finding out where new doors lead.

And so two years ago I shut the door marked work. I left my job and opened the door called University. There I found a magical new world of challenges, opportunities and occasional disappointments. Since then I have open many new doors, some I didn't even know existed.

This collection celebrates that. A few of the poems have been in anthologies, many have been given life on stage with the Poetry Vandals, but most appear for the first time.

Turn the handle and come inside.

Jeff Price

Contents

Page number

Fifteen Doors

In my dreams there are doors
In houses I do not recognise
Leading to rooms I do not know
My house is full of doors
Looking as if they lead somewhere
But most just hide the confusion

Fifteen doors but only seven rooms
Some doors have been moved
Mysteriously relocating themselves
Ashamed of the clutter that lies behind
They bear the marks of abuse
Rejected as well as slammed

One hundred and fifty years
They have been hanging around
Thick, dependable and not very bright
Cracked from over stimulation
Many have had radical surgery
Some of them are off their hinges

Dictionary

My father gave me a dictionary
Full of words I did not understand
And could not pronounce
Every vowel was a brawl
Every consonant a skirmish

I learned to love the words
That I could not spell
To explore their meanings
Tasting their sound on my tongue
Prising them apart
Stitching them back together

In my head I wrote poetry
Furtive words about secrets
Never daring to put pen to paper
In case my words would be mocked
Ridiculed
West End boys don't write poetry

Thirty years ago
On a Routemaster bus in London
Going from Hackney to Stepney
I shared a dictionary with a conductor
We drooled over the pages
Like schoolboys ogling porn

I realised I was not alone
This was not a fetish
Just a fascination for phonetics
Now I let the software
Worry about the spelling
While I enjoy creating the lines

The Ghost Fleet

The engine labours coughs and splutters
The bilge pumps must never stop
She is holed below the Plimsoll line
Taking in damaged water

In port she can be a lively boat
Decked out in bunting
Painted white from stem to stern
She embraces her passengers

At sea she plots her own course
Staying beyond the bar for months
Riding out the storms
Ever watchful of the undertow

In unfamiliar bays they meet
The sister ship's ghost boats
Swapping survival stories
Tall tales of the high seas

The ghost fleet talks bridge to bridge
You can hear the words on the wind
In the chatter of Morse code
Tapping like a blind man's cane

Tales of Captains who promised safe passage
Then abandoned them to the elements
Ship fitters who guaranteed repairs
But could never stop the constant leakage

From the brutish engines of experience
They create stories and poetry
Fashioned in the uncharted seas
Far beyond the sanctuary of ports

Navigating between the lamp and the lea
A precious cargo of verb noun and adjective
Damaged, just trying to stay afloat
They sail on...

Have you got lions on your gateposts?

There are many people who have less than me

No one has died of hunger in my family
At least if they did it was a long time ago
I remember stories from my childhood
About the days before the welfare state
Where Mothers died on kitchen tables
And a rusty blade could eat you alive

But not anymore

The water that I drink does not have to come from a bottle
I don't have to walk five miles to find a tap
If I am hungry it is because I choose not to eat
At night I sleep in a bed that costs
The equivalent of a year's wage for a tea picker
Having no son does not condemn me to poverty in my old age

There are many people who have more than me

I do not own a 42 inch flat screen plasma television
I have no IPOD or 8 megapixel digital camera
If I had a driveway there would no SUV parked on it
If I had gateposts there would be no lions

Are you poor because I am better off than you?
Are you rich because I have less than you?
If the rich had less would the poor have more?
I used to have the answer but I don't know any more

The Invigilator

The students sulk into the room
Stumbling between the desks
"Who has a mobile phone?"
Slowly like bread rising
The hands are raised
We collect the phones.

"Who doesn't have a pen?"
More hands are raised
I hand out pens
Someone else hands out chocolate
The chocolate is more popular than the pens

A student in a Burberry cap raises his hand
He points to the word "Difference"
And asks what it means
Another wants to know what
A "Mean Average" is?

I can't tell them
It's against the Invigilator's code
And if they don't know
Then there wasn't a lot of point
In turning up in the first place

I was like them forty years ago
Couldn't be bothered
I thought it was all a stupid waste of time

Some, after a cursory look at the paper
And twenty minutes of scribbling
Rest their arms on the desk and fall asleep

Now I know
What the point is and why I should be bothered
But I can't tell them that
They're asleep

Later the sleeping students are thanked
For their thoughtfulness
In not disturbing those
Who knew more than they did

Prague

Thirty years ago the walls of Prague were stained
Rubbed cold by neglect and bureaucratic torpor
In those long lost days we ate
In a restaurant at the top of Wenceslas Square
At the end of a long corridor of stoical buildings
We dined in the shadow of the museum
Feasting on goulash thick with dumplings
Washed down with steins of Pilsner beer
We watched waiters laden with courses
Desserts starters and main meals served in random order

Outside the diners cars were held hostage by two Zil Motorcars
The drivers waiting patiently talking to the chauffeurs
As Party officials held court in a sectioned off dining area
In the back streets behind corrugated iron gates Soviets tanks
slumbered
The young people banged their fists on the doors
Surreptitiously slipping flowers from inside their coats
Marking the spot were friends had fallen and comrades fought

Today the Vandals returned to Prague marching in to the radio
station
To the place were Dubcek and Havel had lifted the eyes of the
People
Free to recite poetry that remembers the sacrifices of the past
Looking out on strip clubs Irish Bars and Marks and Spencer
But you only have to lift your eyes a little
To see that the splendour of the city remains intact
Buildings vibrant and as eclectic as a wedding parade
Reminding us of Prague's glory and assuring its future
The Zils have gone replaced by the SUV's of the noveau riche
The restaurant at the top of Wenceslas Square
Has been replaced with the golden arches of McDonalds
Capitalism mixed rough with Hapsburg and Art Noveau grandeur
Rubbing uncomfortable shoulders with hope and freedom

Thirty years ago Prague seemed to be in a fetid sleep
Today the chatter of every nation clatters on the cobbles
The arc lamps of the night illuminating its majestic buildings
The city is writing another chapter of its turbulent and fabulous
history

Grandfather's Visit

Last night my Grandfather dropped in for a visit
I had not seen his smile in nearly forty years
I was asleep, he did not say anything
Just to see his half forgotten face was enough

It was a warm October afternoon when I last saw him
In the front room of my Auntie's house in Heaton
He called out to my Grandma to bring us some tea
Which never arrived, she had died long before I was
born

Lost between the past and the present he was
running out of time
Merciful nature had made fresh his ninety years of
memories
Last night before fitful sleep I had been thinking of a
lost friend
My Grandfather was reminding me wherever he is he
has not forgotten me

When my time comes and I sit with my Grandson
calling for tea
And the past and the present merge into one stream
of time
I will relive each second of my life, savouring my
memories
Like a pint slipping effortlessly down my throat at the
end of a working week

Fries with that

The outlook is good, the future's brighter
I trying to make a living as a poet and a writer
The literary world has shown me the welcome mat
Can I ask, "Do you want fries with that?"

It's not easy, you have to take some chances
Causing problems with your shaky finances
To all those friends whose warnings fell flat
Can I ask, "Do you want fries with that?"

They told me a book would make me a mint
But the publishers have a backlog waiting to print
There is fuck all chance of growing fat
Can I ask, "Do you want fries with that?"

I have work teaching poetry in a school
It just two hours next month in Hartlepool
I don't want to sound like a spoilt brat
Can I ask, "Do you want fries with that?"

I have a fall back, in case you haven't guessed
If everything doesn't work out for the best
I am standing in an apron, wearing a paper hat
Can I ask, "Do you want fries with that?"

A World Away

Perfidious winter began in a flash
Holding the fragile world in its grip
December winds cutting like a lash
Splintered like an abandoned ship

Storms sweeping from all directions
Uprooting the husbandry of forty years
Replacing order with devastation
Biting back cold words, empty tears

At first the snow is as slow as a snail to leave
Cold and damp as a crowded tomb
There is no warmth on this winters eve
No welcome of crocuses from spring's womb

The storm passes, the wind whimper's home
In the milky dawn the sun breaks
In the compost fresh shoots are growing
New life and hope makes its debut

The Earth must be replenished and renewed
Winters finger's must give way to spring
The efficacious Sun will find its sting

Before spring winter must have its say
Sweet summer is still a world away

The Mayfair

When I was young and became a man
I danced through the night
In her glittering sweat stained rooms
On that darkened dance floor
Of golden and silver light

Now, they are to pull it down
So you can park your car
Drive carefully because
You're parked on my dreams

With apologies to W B Yeats

Cold Comfort

The snow sits idly on the kitchen roof
Swept down on artic winds from Siberia
It waits for the warm westerly wind
Then slips away like a reluctant guest at a party

The snow of my childhood lasted for weeks
Bringing with it my Grandfather
The steep streets of Willington Quay
Too severe for his uncertain legs

In Fenham we would walk the pavements together
Secure in his place by my side, we became allies
He was safe from icy inclines
I, protected from my Father's vengeful hands

Hooks

You could not see the banister
At the bottom of the stairs
For coats scarves and hats

Coats left behind on summer nights
Hats from cold winter days
Scarves refugees from autumn storms

It's not easy going upstairs
Without coats scarves and hats
Tumbling on to the floor

I bought two sets of hooks
Drilled holes in the wall
Screwed them in to place

Hung up the coats scarves and hats
In the morning they were in a heap
On the floor

The weight of the coats scarves and hats
Had been too much
Ripping the hooks off the wall

Now the plaster is cracked
The wallpaper ragged and torn
Hooks bent and broken

Relocating your problems
Resolves nothing

Once a Catholic

I was born into the Catholic Church
The catechism beaten into me
A steel forged blade on a Roman anvil
Faith seeps from even the most devoted
A slow puncture on the road of life
Hardly noticed over the years
Then routine and the fear of the hereafter
Keep them shackled to the Altar

But for me
My faith was involved in a head on shunt
On a spring morning when I was thirteen
I was an Alter boy for Father Boyle
Saying mass in an empty chapel
He rattled through like an express train
Never stopping at the stations in between
Only focused on getting to the end
He ignored obstructions
Pausing only to issue instructions to me
As the final bell rang he checked his watch
Eleven and a half minutes
And with a triumphant smile
He announced his personal best time
A light went on in my mind
It was just a game to him
That meant nothing to me
My belief hitched a ride
On the breakdown truck
I waved it goodbye
I have never seen it again
In the years that followed
On dark crisis ridden nights
When all hope seemed gone
I would call up an instinctive prayer
That was always unanswered
Slowly the icy hand of the past weakened its grip
Thirty years have passed since the last prayer left my
lips

My Father spent most of his 84 years
Commuting between home and Church
It would have pleased him
If one of his four sons had become a Priest
Towards the end of his life
He would have settled for
One of his children going to church
I wonder if his faith ever wavered?
Did he ever meet his Father Boyle?

I read the sermon at my father's funeral
Not because I believed in the words
But because he did

Left Luggage

You found the suitcase left by a lover
I locked the trunk against betrayal
I gave you the rucksack full of misgiving and doubts
You gave me a valise of ghostly memories
We have five carrier bags of bruised cosmetics

We have filled the house with baggage
Jammed in the hallway like the homeless
I need to push the door hard when I want to come in

Wet behind the ears

I have thrown myself off the cliff plunging not flying
No way back to the safe secure upper world
Below I see the water rushing towards me
Stomach nerves knotted and toes curled

I am a snake oil salesman who has slipped his skin
Recently demobbed from the rat race
I signed up for a tour of duty in Academe
Hopeful that I can hack the work and stand the pace

I am wet behind my student ears
Keen as a butcher's blade to succeed
Striding through the September rain
No looking back to watch the past recede

First Day Back

My suntan is fading fast
On my first day back
I slip on my wrist watch
Hastily retrieved from my holiday hold-all
Where it has lain unmourned
For seven sun soaked days

My skin peels like damp wallpaper
As dried out
As my enthusiasm for work
Each scratchy snowflake
Reminds me of the long months
Before I am once again
Under my holiday tree
With a cold beer in my hand
Half a novel still to read

Baggage

I brought a small holdall on holiday
A few tee-shirts
Minimum toiletries
I left the rest of my baggage
Behind in the hallway
It's not that I don't care
I only left them behind
Confident in the knowledge
That they will still be there
On my return

Public Notice

I have noticed
Your Notices
And your concern
For the things
You notice

I notice them too
But it doesn't
Bother me
Like it does
You

Someone leaves
A can of paint
Washing has been left too long
Sounds bleed through walls

In the rubbish room
An abandoned television
Offends no-one
Except your eye

I smell tobacco
And Tandoori vapours
In the corridors
It's my neighbours
I find it comforting
You it affronts

Take my advice
Get a life

I have driven too long

I have driven too many miles
Peering through the swirling snow
I watch distracted
The road shimmers in front
A stress fracture opens up in my brain
An eighteen wheeler tries to side swipe me
In my anger
I decided to immortalise the trucker
In a devastating poem
Thick with pungent irony
But I am so tired
I cannot even find a rhyme for...

The bastard driver of the oil tanker

Black and White

When I was a youth
Crammed into the piss stained
Terrace of the Leazes End
At St James Park
I carried a rattle
Made by a long forgotten Uncle

At the top of it's wooden stem
Was an oblong of slats
Painted black and white
That rattled off machine gun fire
When it was spun above my head

In those days everything was black and white
No shades of compromising grey

Today I listen to the other person's point of view
Consider with respect their alternative ideas
Except were football is concerned
There everything is still black and white

Total Eclipse

There are no towels in a sodden heap on the bathroom floor
There is no trail of discarded clothes leading to her bedroom
There are no abandoned tubes of make up and eyebrow pencils
There are no small pieces of toilet paper in front of the mirror

The phone has stopped ringing every five minutes
The doorbell no longer buzzes at two in the morning
The kitchen is tidy. the fridge is full of food
The bath is clean, my razor has no legs to shave

No one has forgotten their front door key
No one wants dropping off at a friend's house
No one is smoking in her bedroom
No one is demanding money with menaces

My Daughter has gone to watch the eclipse
Her corona is obscured by distance
But she will come back again soon
To illuminate the corners of my world

A Row of Tents

I cross my legs sitting in a chair
I have never had an extramarital affair
When I go down town I wear a jacket
I count the change in my pay packet

I go to the theatre more often than a club
Can't drink more than four pints in the pub
I like to cook and make my own bread
Occasionally I get out of my head

I've got no body piercing, earrings or tattoo
I read the sports section after the Arts revue
At a party I can strut, I can dance
My motto is "let's give quiche a chance"

I will write you a poem, a stanza or two
I don't eat meat, never been to a zoo
I think the middle classes are overtaxed
I've been known to get my eyebrows waxed

I've never worn a Newcastle United top
I am glad that hunting got the chop
I can keep a secret and I can be discreet
I've shed a tear watching Coronation Street

It doesn't mean I can't be hard or tough
I can take the smooth with the rough
I'm a Geordie who walks his own line
A renaissance man from Newcastle on Tyne

West End

The West End of the city has no
Theatres or Harrods shopping
Families have fled from it's
Once thriving streets
With summer life on the step
They are now the playground
Of the car thief
The sullen burglar's dog

Charred sandstone window sills
Boarded against the vandals
Have been gutted of worth
Fired by abandoned youths
And greedy landlords
Eager to reap an insured crop

The shops are deserted
Robbed and intimidated
Beyond the endurance of
The nation of shopkeepers
Napoleon feared

Only the closing down sale
Of the camping supply shop
Marks the dying days that declare
Now is the winter of our discount tents

No-Mans Land

We make love in No-Mans land
Amongst the shrapnel of our mistakes
Frightened, exposed and vulnerable

We retreat to our fortified trenches
Terrified that we will be caught
In the cross hairs of a snipers rifle

Nana

Every Friday Nana came
The few staggered steps
To our Catholic door
Bringing my copy of the Eagle
To the ritual fish & chip supper

I would consume the tales
of Dan Dare and the Mighty Mekon
With greater relish than any
Six penny worth and
A battered Haddock or Cod

Be My Valentine

Be my Valentine, be my eternal love
Although you should know
That I have issues with Woman
Due to unresolved trauma
Caused by a domineering Mother
And the lack of a Father figure in my early years
Whilst I am happy to see you from time to time
I am unable to enter into a more permanent
relationship
As I have trouble with the concept of commitment
And see it as an interference with my personal space

Four by Four

In my living room
Four teenage girls talk
Conducting a complex matrix
Of interwoven conversations

In the corner of the room
The television demands attention
I ask them politely
To turn it fucking down

Amy tells me it is impossible
She is watching the Simpsons
How can she watch television
And talk to three different people?

My daughter informs me
That woman can do this easily
I know better than
To quibble with her

You can not argue
With an article of faith
It forms an integral part
Of her feminist catechism

Passed down
From Mother to Daughter
As holy writ
Since the nineteen eighties

I retreat to the bathroom
Wallow in warm water
Turn on the radio
Tune out the voices

Sober Nights

Now we have drunk the last barrel dry
Toasted those great nights
Of listening to fabulous music
And watching drunken fights
I think about drinking
The years of bodily abuse
I'm not a stupid person
I shouldn't make an excuse
For my aching drinkers bladder
My throbbing drinkers head
Those Monday mornings
It was hard to get out of bed
Words I shouldn't have uttered
Nights I should have gone home
Songs I should never have sung
Those hours talking on the phone
I would look and feel a lot better
My waist and arse wouldn't sag
I could jog for miles in the morning
Probably manage a decent shag
If I never have another pint
Or smoked another joint
I might live till I'm eighty
But what's the fucking point

Three Little Words

I am the poet
Who shapes sentences
Like a potter moulds clay
Creating malleable lines

I am the poet
Who stands before his peers
And speaks from the heart
With seeming confidence

There are some words
I find it impossible to say
Stillborn in my mouth
Unable to find a way out

As a young child
I have no memory of my parents
Saying those words to me
Although I know they loved me

And over the intervening years
Those words came back cold
So I stopped using them
I want to say them to you

Those three little words
That short sentence
That catch on the
Scar tissue of the past

So instead one night in bed
In the soft stillness of the night
I will say "I vole you"
It's not enough but it's a start

Dolphin Girl

The ragged voices
Surround her
Words clash and bend
Flapping like washing in the wind
Finding their stumbling feat
Drumming out the erratic beat

Centre stage
She sits
Hands clasped
They are the words
She is the sound of the Gods
She is passion
The heart of pleasure
Essence of understanding

Dancers crack the wave
Pulsing across the stage
Rising to the pull of her sound
Crashing down again
Tails arcing water
Her voice
Escalating with the movement
Delighting in the twists
Twisting in the wind

Her sisters call
Click, Click
She broadcasts
They listen
Sharing her pleasure
So many said so much
She said everything
Never uttering a word

Facts like Figs

She picks facts like figs
Arranging them in patterns
That serve her purpose

Gulp Gone

Gulp gulp gone
Swallowed
Forgotten
One small stone
Two new stones
A handful
Stomach full
Grit gulp gulp
Your small stone
Protecting
Gravel gulp
Week month year
Gravel gulp
More stones
More people
Stone scree scree
Slide slide grasp
Fall fall tear
Scrabble scree
Lose footing
Goodbye
Gone

Making contact with Day

I am blindfolded in the morning
Stumbling into the world like a drunken puppy
I see colour and shape but no detail
Shaking off the night running aground from sleep to
shore
Shower shave and shift uncomfortably on the toilet
Razor scraping off foam like snow from a windscreen
I am booted and suited brushed and clean
Shirt ironed tie straitened
With my hands tied behind my back
Kettle coffee mug and milk
White on the right blue on the left

Not Guilty

The man who gave you the sack
The man who never called you back
It wasn't me

The man who started the war
The man who called you a whore
It wasn't me

The man who stopped you voting
The man you thought revolting
It wasn't me

The man who wanted you to iron his shirt
The man who treated you like dirt
It wasn't me

The man who wanted you to be his Mother
The man who was a crappy lover
It wasn't me

The man who never said goodbye
The man who made you cry
It wasn't me

Just because I have a penis
Isn't a difference between us
I am not from Mars
And you're not from Venus

Poetry Nights

There's a roach or two scurrying across the floor
A pile of old newspapers stacked up behind the door
A three legged chair left from a drunken fight
A stack of empty bottles from Friday's girls night

There's the remains of the buffet no one wanted to
eat
A lumpy old settee that should be tossed into the
street
Some cheese and chilli crisps that no one wants to
try
A stack of Poetry Vandals CD's that no one wants to
buy

There's some Socialist Worker flyers about the Iraqi
war
An invitation to see a group that no one has heard of
before
We sit here in silence and contemplate the futility of
it all
How we put posters around the colleges, in all the
student halls

Adverts on the radio, articles in the local rags
We dressed up the stage, hung out the flags
I tell you what it is, the thing I struggle to
understand
Why there's nobody here but poets and someone
from the band

Trotsky

The once shining statue
Has been painted black
Torn from its plinth
And cast to the ground
History has been rewritten
Dates have been altered
Words erased from the files
New documents inserted
Soon there will be little left
Of those once glorious times
I was Trotsky
Now I am Stalin

Looking for Clues

As the soft morning light drifts in
I feel her search my soul with her eyes
She thumbs through my mind for clues
She needs to know
If I came too early
Or she came too late

Lourdes

On the street the garish gift shops
Dispense plastic Madonnas
Flick knives and forgiveness
Processions of the lame and infirm
Snake there way towards the shrine
Hoping that there will be hope
Where there is no hope
I feel the tug of my upbringing
An affinity with the huddled queue
I think of lighting a candle for my Father
And realise it means nothing to me
Accept a vague sense of loss and regret

Warwick Street

Cracked and crazy students
Crammed in four by fours
Stamping on the carpetless floor
Late night slamming of car doors
Disgusting stains on a stiffened sheet
In a student flat on Warwick Street

Late night chorus of Eskimo Nell
Giving the old age pensioners hell
Dropping the pizza all over the bed
Bank account in the red
Nothing is kept tidy or neat
By the students of Warwick Street

An occasional visit to the Lecture Hall
Throwing up at the student Ball
They smoke Marlboro and Tack
Never take their empties back
Life for them is always indiscreet
The pampered students of Warwick Street

In three short years they will be gone
But the memory will linger on
Every day a treat
On scruffy unsanitary spew stained
Warwick Street

Apologies to John Cooper Clarke

Closing Time

I thought I would drink with him
Late into a Newcastle night
Smoking our troubles
Chewing the fat on steak and rumours
Telling tales of Gallic footballers
Firing brickbats across the bar

He understanding my language
Better than I did

Me responding by accusing the French
Of hijacking our nouns and adjectives

He had the chance to order another pint
But, for reasons I will never understand
He waited too long
And by then...

Closing time had been called

For Gerard Mace

Crossing Cultural Divides

She sailed two years ago
Bagged up to the gunnels
Following in Cook's wake
A journey into the known

She plotted her course
Courtesy of the Rough Guide
Flying in to the rising sun
Mapping out new territories

Seeking out ancient landscapes
Crossing cultural divides
Working her passage
Working her ticket

She has taken Geordie culture
To the land Down Under
She posts pissed pictures
Of Christmas day on the beach

Moments of time captured
In Maori shopping Malls
Melon farms, food factories
Samoa, Fiji, the Cook Islands

In a car that cost less than a shirt
Driving down the spine of the South Island
She finds the end of the world
And a friend she went to school with

I am stalking her on the internet
Googling her destinations
Checking out the webcams
I have become a virtual Father

DIY Redemption

My God is white, yours is black
My God is patriotic, he has a Union Jack
My God is tall and yours is small
My God wants you to live behind a wall
My God thinks your religion is trash
My God needs lots of cash
My God tells me to throw bombs at you
My God is Catholic, yours is a Jew
My God will repress you and make me free
My God thinks your ideas are a threat to me
My God supports my politics, despising yours
My God has an army, he fights lots of wars
My God is orange, yours is green
My God is compassionate, yours is obscene

Only the one God but each is home grown
Take your prejudices and create your own

Acknowledgements

This book is dedicated to my wife Lynda.

She opened many doors for me and because of her support I was able to leave my job in the computer industry and spend a year as a student at Newcastle University. So many good things have flowed from that time.

Special thanks to Poetry Vandals Annie Moir and Kate Fox for their help in editing and proofing the book.

Thanks also to the rest of the Poetry Vandals (Aidan, Karl and Scott) who have always been a source of support and inspiration.

There have been many others who have encouraged and supported me; Chris Moir, Kevin Cadwallender, Nev Clay, Jo and Michael at the Cumberland, Fred Plater, George Hendricks, Dharma Banana and many more too numerous to mention...Thank you...

Last but not least (in age order)

Emma, Hester, Suzi, Amy and Madeleine